The Assassination of John F. Kennedy

Death of the New Frontier

KAREN PRICE HOSSELL

Heinemann

www.heinemann.co.uk/library
Visit our website to find out more information about **Heinemann Library** books.

To order:
☎ Phone 44 (0) 1865 888066
▤ Send a fax to 44 (0) 1865 314091
▢ Visit the Heinemann Bookshop at www.heinemann.co.uk/library to browse our catalogue and order online.

First published in Great Britain by Heinemann Library, Halley Court, Jordan Hill, Oxford OX2 8EJ, a division of Reed Educational and Professional Publishing Ltd. Heinemann is a registered trademark of Reed Educational & Professional Publishing Limited.

OXFORD MELBOURNE AUCKLAND JOHANNESBURG BLANTYRE
GABORONE IBADAN PORTSMOUTH NH (USA) CHICAGO

Designed by Roslyn Broder
Originated by Dot Gradations Limited
Printed and bound at Lake Book Manufacturing

ISBN 0 431 06726 0 (hardback)
06 05 04 03 02
10 9 8 7 6 5 4 3 2 1

British Library Cataloguing in Publication Data

Hossell, Karen Price
  Assassination of John F. Kennedy: death of the new frontier - (Turning points in history)
  1. Kennedy, John F. (John Fitzgerald), 1917-1963 - Assassination - Juvenile literature
  I. Title
  973.9'22'092

Acknowledgements
The Publishers would like to thank the following for permission to reproduce photographs:
pp. 4, 7, 8, 9, 14, 15, 20, 21, 22, 23, 25, 26 Bettmann/Corbis; pp. 5, 10, 17 Corbis; p. 6 Flip Schulke/Corbis; pp. 11, 16, 18 AP/Wide World Photos; p. 12 Hulton-Deutsch Collection/Corbis; p. 19 William A. Bake/Corbis; p. 27 Wally McNamee/Corbis; p. 28 NASA; p. 29 Rob Rowan, Progressive Image/Corbis.

Cover photograph by (T-B): Bettmann/Corbis; AP/Wide World Photos.

Every effort has been made to contact copyright holders of any material reproduced in this book. Any omissions will be rectified in subsequent printings if notice is given to the Publishers.

Contents

Some words are shown in bold, **like this.** You can find out what they mean by looking in the Glossary.

The murder of a president

On 21 November 1963, the president of the United States, John Fitzgerald Kennedy, and his wife, Jacqueline, flew to the state of Texas. With them were the vice-president, former Texas senator Lyndon B. Johnson, and his wife. They went to the Texan cities of San Antonio and Fort Worth, then flew to Dallas on 22 November, where the president was scheduled to speak at a lunch.

President and Mrs Kennedy rode to this appointment in an open-topped car with Texas governor John B. Connally and his wife. A limousine full of **Secret Service** agents followed them for protection, and Vice-president Johnson and his wife rode in another limousine behind the Secret Service car. The cars formed a sort of parade called a motorcade.

ALL THE WAY WITH J.F.K.

People lined the streets of Dallas, Texas, to see the handsome president and glamorous first lady.

Tragedy strikes

Kennedy smiled and waved at the crowd as the motorcade slowly drove through the streets of Dallas. Then the president suddenly grabbed his neck and leaned over, as though he was in pain. Seconds later, he fell into his wife's lap. The crowd did not know what had happened, but the driver of the president's car and the vehicles following it increased their speed and raced away.

The president had been shot twice – once in the neck and once in the head – and Governor Connally, who was sitting in front of the president, had also been shot. The motorcade travelled directly to nearby Parkland Hospital with the injured men. The president's injuries were so severe that doctors could do nothing to save him. At one o'clock – 30 minutes after he was shot – the president was pronounced dead. Governor Connally was badly injured as well, but he would survive.

The news spreads

All over the United States people heard the news. Wives called their husbands at work to tell them the president had been shot. Teachers were called into corridors, then went back into the classroom to tell their pupils the sad news. Then more information came. Television stations interrupted regular programming to announce that President Kennedy was dead.

Many people across the world felt their lives were changed forever by the assassination of President Kennedy.

The country and the world were shocked. The 46-year-old president, father of two young children, was gone. Schools let their students go home early. People sobbed in the streets. Even Walter Cronkite, a man millions of Americans had watched deliver the news on television for years without becoming emotional, had to hold back tears as he told the country. For a day, everything stopped. When things started up again, they would never be the same. A time of peace, innocence and wealth would move towards a time of **unrest**, greater awareness of social problems and increased involvement in a foreign war in far-off Vietnam.

Post-war America

The 1950s were a time of economic success for many Americans. After World War II ended in 1945, many **veterans** went to college, got married and had children. More affordable homes were being built and new technology was making life easier for everyone. Most women did not work outside the home and they had new appliances to make their housework easier, including dishwashers, air conditioners and electric sewing machines. In the evenings, families gathered around the television to watch programmes about happy, middle-class families.

Martin Luther King Jr, a 27-year-old activist, led a bus **boycott** in Montgomery, Alabama, in 1956 to protest against segregation in transport.

Inequality

But not everyone in the United States lived this way. African Americans were rarely seen on television or in films in the 1950s. People were **segregated** – separated by race – in many areas of life, including education and public transport.

In 1954, the United States **Supreme Court** ruled in the court case *Brown versus Board of Education* that it was **unconstitutional** to segregate students in state schools. Schools were told to start to **desegregate**, but there was violent opposition to the changes from many whites.

The Cold War

The United States had problems at home such as racial **unrest**, but the country also had to face the worldwide problem of the **Cold War**. This was not an actual war, but was a conflict of ideas between the two greatest powers in the world about how governments should be run.

One power was the United States and its allies, or friends, called the West. The other was the **Soviet Union** and its allies, called the East. The Cold War began soon after World War II ended in 1945.

The main reason for the conflict between these two groupings was their differing ideas of how a nation should be governed. The Soviet Union and its supporters believed that **communism** was the best way to run a country, while the United States was – and still is – a **democracy**. Each power feared attack from the other, and also feared the other was planning to take over more countries. As a result of these fears, the United States and the Soviet Union built up their stocks of nuclear weapons.

During the Cold War, some Americans built shelters as a place to hide in the event of a nuclear bomb attack.

BLACKLISTING

In the 1950s and 1960s, fear of communism led to the persecution of Americans merely suspected of being sympathetic to communism. Many people, including Hollywood writers, film and television stars, university lecturers and people in trade unions, were accused of being communists or of attending communist meetings. After the accusations, they became blacklisted. This meant that their names were published in newspapers and they were criticized on the streets and in business meetings. Many employers refused to hire blacklisted people.

John F. Kennedy

John F. Kennedy was born in Brookline, Massachusetts, in 1917. Both sides of his family were involved in politics. His father's father was a state senator. His mother's father, John F. Fitzgerald, was a state senator, a United States Congressman and the mayor of the largest city in Massachusetts, Boston. Kennedy's father, Joseph P. Kennedy, was a US **ambassador** to the United Kingdom and a businessman who became a millionaire.

Kennedy took command of the patrol boat *PT 109* on 23 April 1943.

War hero

John F. Kennedy (usually known as Jack) graduated from Harvard University in 1940. He joined the US Navy during World War II and was assigned to a PT (patrol torpedo boat) – a small, fast fighting ship. In August 1943, his boat was patrolling off the Solomon Islands in the South Pacific when it was cut in two by a Japanese ship. Two men were killed and the ten other men on board, including Kennedy, clung to wreckage all night. The next morning, they sighted an island and Kennedy ordered everyone to swim to it. Even though Kennedy's back was badly hurt, he helped another injured man swim to the island. They were rescued several days later. Kennedy received a Navy and Marine Corps Medal for his heroism and a Purple Cross for being wounded in combat.

Public figure

After the war, Kennedy was elected to the US House of Representatives. He served as a Democratic congressman for Massachusetts from 1947 to 1952. In 1952, he was elected to a seat in the US Senate.

Kennedy's wartime back injury began to bother him more and more, so he had two operations, one in

1954 and another in 1955. While he was recovering, Kennedy wrote a book called *Profiles in Courage*. In 1957, he won the prestigious Pulitzer Prize, an important American award given to only a few writers each year, for the book.

Presidential campaign

In 1956, Kennedy decided he would run for president in the 1960 election. Many people thought it would be a problem that Kennedy was a Roman Catholic. Only one other Roman Catholic had ever been **nominated** for president, and he had lost the election. Some people also thought Kennedy was too young. If he won, he would become president at only 43, making him the youngest person ever to be president. His Republican opponent was Richard M. Nixon, who was the serving vice-president under Dwight D. Eisenhower, and was associated with the wartime generation.

Kennedy was nominated to run for president at the 1960 Democratic National Convention. His youthful energy and ideals appealed to a new generation of voters.

A FUTURE OF CHALLENGES

As Kennedy **campaigned** for president, he put together a programme he called 'The New Frontier'. Kennedy accepted the Democratic Party's nomination for president by making a speech about his goals for the New Frontier. The following extract is taken from his speech:

'We stand today on the edge of a New Frontier – the frontier of the 1960s – a frontier of unknown opportunities and perils – a frontier of unfulfilled hopes and threats... But the New Frontier of which I speak is not a set of promises – it is a set of challenges. It sums up not what I intend to offer the American people, but what I intend to ask of them... But I tell you the New Frontier is here, whether we seek it or not. Beyond that frontier are the uncharted areas of science and space, unsolved problems of peace and war, unconquered pockets of ignorance and prejudice, unanswered questions of poverty and surplus.'

The New Frontier

The 1960 debates

In 1960, Kennedy decided to use television in a way no other presidential candidate ever had. He challenged Richard M. Nixon to a series of four televised **debates**. Nixon's advisers told him not to do it, because he was ahead in the polls and was expected to win the election anyway. But he wanted to debate with Kennedy, so he agreed to go on television.

The television debate between Kennedy (left) and Nixon (not pictured) had a dramatic effect on election results.

On the night of the first debate, Nixon was pale and thin, because he had just spent time in hospital recovering from a knee injury. He also had what is called a five-o'clock shadow – his face looked unshaven even though he had recently shaved. In contrast, Kennedy was tan and healthy looking. During the debates he appeared cool and confident, while Nixon was sweaty and seemed nervous. Those who heard the debates on the radio thought Nixon did a better job, but those who saw them on television pronounced Kennedy the winner. And indeed, Kennedy did go on to win the election, but only by about 120,000 **popular votes**.

The New Frontier platform

Kennedy's 'New Frontier' **platform** had many goals. They included a higher **minimum wage**, medical care for the elderly, increased **federal** aid for education, **legislation** for **civil rights**, improved life in cities and major tax cuts. Kennedy also wanted to 'win' the **Cold War** by spending more money on weapons. The goals of increased minimum wages and increased spending on weapons were achieved, but many of his other goals were not. One reason was that **Congress** was not ready to pass some of his **reforms**. Another reason was that he did not push to get legislation passed, particularly legislation about civil rights.

Kennedy planned to prepare Congress for his new ideas during his first four-year presidential term so that when he ran again – and won – in 1964, his reforms would be passed. To be re-elected, Kennedy would need the votes of Southern Democrats, and many in the South were against civil rights. Most of the time he was in office, President Kennedy simply tried to **enforce** the existing civil rights laws.

Neighbourhoods, such as this street in New York, were part of the focus of Kennedy's New Frontier. He wanted to reduce poverty levels and bring up the standard of living for many Americans.

A CALL TO SERVICE

On 20 January 1961, the day of his **inauguration** as president, Kennedy spoke these words in his speech. He called upon his audience to help make the world a better place:

'In your hands, my fellow citizens, more than in mine, will rest the final success or failure of our course. Since this country was founded, each generation of Americans has been summoned to give testimony to its national loyalty. The graves of young Americans who answered the call to service surround the globe. Now the trumpet summons us again – not as a call to bear arms, though arms we need; not as a call to battle, though embattled we are – but a call to bear the burden of a long twilight struggle, year in and year out, 'rejoicing in hope, patient in tribulation' – a struggle against the common enemies of man: tyranny, poverty, disease and war itself.'

The 35th president

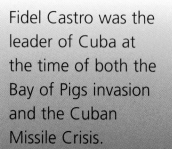

The Peace Corps

One of Kennedy's first actions after becoming president was to create the Peace Corps. This organization came to represent his 'New Frontier', with its goal of promoting world peace and friendship. Volunteers help in areas such as education and healthcare, and learn how other people live. The Peace Corps is still active, and more than 150,000 Americans have been volunteers.

The Bay of Pigs invasion

Kennedy was forced to deal with two incidents involving Cuba while he was president. The first incident was the Bay of Pigs invasion, which took place in April 1961, soon after he was elected. The US **Central Intelligence Agency (CIA)** had trained Cuban **exiles** – people who had left Cuba to live in the United States – to overthrow Cuba's **communist** government. Unfortunately, the invasion did not go as planned. Cuban aeroplanes bombed American ships, and CIA boats were wrecked on a coral reef. Local Cubans were there to meet the invaders when they landed and held them until the Cuban army arrived. About 1100 of the 1400 invaders were captured and 114 died.

Fidel Castro was the leader of Cuba at the time of both the Bay of Pigs invasion and the Cuban Missile Crisis.

Divided Berlin

In August 1961, Kennedy was faced with another foreign problem. A wall was built, totally cutting off the western section of the German city of Berlin from the rest of the city. Known as the 'Berlin Wall', it became a symbol of the repression of the people of eastern Europe. Throughout his presidency, Kennedy supported the citizens of Berlin. He made the whole world listen to his views on the subject when he gave a now-famous speech in July 1963 in the shadow of the Berlin Wall. He said that if people did not understand the difference between the free and communist world, '*Let them come to Berlin*'.

The Cuban Missile Crisis

In October 1962, there was another problem in Cuba. US spy planes flying over Cuba saw missile sites being set up with these weapons aimed at the United States. A plane photographed the sites and US intelligence agencies studied the photographs. The agencies soon verified that Cuba and the **Soviet Union** were setting up nuclear missiles in Cuba. Kennedy and his advisers thought long and hard about this **Cold War** threat to the United States. They considered an air strike or an invasion, but finally settled on a **naval blockade** of Cuba. Ships from the US Navy surrounded the island country and stopped any other ships from going in or coming out.

THE SPACE PROGRAMME

On 12 April 1961, the Soviet Union sent the first man into space – Yuri Gagarin. President Kennedy was interested in space exploration and hoped to see a man on the moon in his lifetime. In a speech to **Congress** on 25 May 1961, he said:

'This nation should commit itself to achieving the goal, before this decade is out, of landing a man on the Moon and returning him safely to Earth. No single space project in this period will be more impressive to mankind, or more important in the long-range exploration of space; and none will be so difficult or expensive to accomplish.'

The United States and the Soviet Union finally settled the issue in November 1962. Kennedy agreed not to invade Cuba and to withdraw US missiles from Turkey, a country near the Soviet Union. Nikita Khrushchev, the leader of the Soviet Union, then agreed to remove Soviet missiles from Cuba. Kennedy's skilful handling of the situation raised his international reputation.

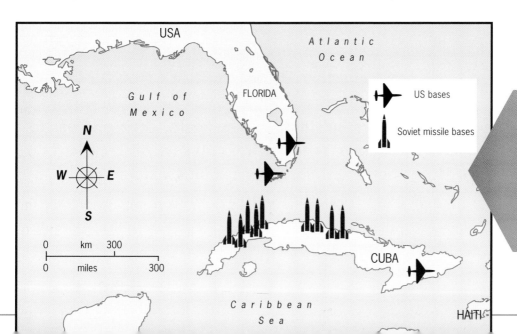

Cuba seemed a serious threat to the United States because it is so close to Florida.

Civil rights and the Cold War

Because the **Cold War** was such an important issue during the late 1950s and early 1960s, Kennedy did not focus much attention on the issue of **civil rights**. But trouble had been brewing for years over racial **injustice**, especially in the South. In 1955 in Montgomery, Alabama, Rosa Parks refused to sit in the back of the bus, as African Americans were required to do by law. Her action led to a bus **boycott** headed by Martin Luther King Jr. In 1957, King formed the Southern Christian Leadership Conference, which worked for civil rights using non-violent means.

Taking a stand

In 1960, four African-American men staged what was called a sit-in at a local café in Greensboro, North Carolina. Because they were black, they were not supposed to sit at the counter, so no one would serve them. They refused to move, however, and sat there for about two hours while white customers were served. More sit-ins took place throughout the South. Then a group of seven African Americans and six white people took a 'Freedom Ride' through the South. Their goal was to break down **segregation** in the national public transport system. The group was attacked by a mob in Rock Hill, South Carolina, and the bus was set on fire just inside the Alabama border. Other groups took freedom rides and met with more violence.

Rosa Parks set progress in motion by taking a brave stand against racism.

These events made President Kennedy turn his attention to the issue of civil rights. After more violence, including the bombing of a church in Birmingham, Alabama, where four African-American girls were killed, he wrote **legislation** that focused on civil rights. His civil rights bill banned racial **discrimination** in public places, prohibited employers and trade unions from discriminating against employees because of race and denied **federal** funds to segregated schools.

LIMITED NUCLEAR TEST BAN TREATY

Because of the Cold War, the United States and the **Soviet Union** tested nuclear bombs in the air, underground and under water. When the bombs and missiles were tested, they caused dangerous **radioactive fallout**. President Eisenhower tried to form an agreement with the Soviet Union to stop the testing. He and Soviet leader Nikita Khrushchev agreed to stop, but no formal agreement was signed. In September 1960, the Soviet Union began testing bombs again, despite the agreement. When President Kennedy discovered this, he allowed the United States to restart testing. After the Cuban Missile Crisis, the two countries decided to stop the tests. In July 1963, the countries reached a formal agreement to stop testing nuclear weapons.

US troops gathered to watch an atomic bomb explode at a test site. Such tests greatly concerned the public.

One day in Dallas

On 22 November 1963, many people in Dallas, Texas, were excited about President Kennedy's visit as part of his political tour. In the city centre, people stopped work to go out on the street or look out of the window to see the president's motorcade drive by. They took pictures to show their children and grandchildren that they had seen the president.

Many Kennedy supporters gathered to greet John and Jackie Kennedy at Dallas airport.

Not everyone was happy that the president was coming to Texas, however. Some people did not like the fact that he came from a wealthy family. They thought the president did not understand what poor people had to go through. Some did not like the president's views on **civil rights**. They wanted African Americans to live, eat, shop and go to school separately, rather than with white people. But even though some people disagreed with Kennedy's politics, most of them wished the president no harm. They knew he had been a hero in World War II and they respected his role as president.

The Assassin

At least one man was there that day specifically to harm President Kennedy. His name was Lee Harvey Oswald, and he had stationed himself at a window in the fifth floor of the Texas School Book Depository building where he worked. As Kennedy's motorcade drove by, Oswald shot at the president using a high-powered rifle. Later that day, Oswald was walking down the street near the boarding house where he lived when a police officer stopped his car, got out and began to question him. The suspected **assassin** shot and killed the police officer, then ran into a nearby cinema to hide. Officers found Oswald there and arrested him.

Two days later, as Oswald was being moved from one jail to another, a man named Jack Ruby stepped out of a crowd of reporters and shot him. Oswald died soon afterward. Ruby said he killed Oswald because he did not want Jacqueline Kennedy to have to sit through a court trial. Many people, however, think Ruby and Oswald were connected, and that Ruby killed Oswald to keep him quiet.

This photograph of Oswald with his rifle was taken in his back garden sometime before the Kennedy **assassination**.

THE END OF CAMELOT

The new president and first lady fascinated even those who were not interested in politics. Some people said that the Kennedy days in the White House were like Camelot – the legendary kingdom of King Arthur – because everything seemed beautiful and everyone was happy. The Kennedys appeared as much like a king and queen as they did a president and first lady. They came from wealthy families, went to the best schools, wore expensive designer clothes and had famous friends, many of them film stars. American women watched closely to see what Jackie Kennedy was wearing and she often started trends in fashion. When Kennedy was killed, this magic time ended.

After the assassination

Vice-president Johnson was at the hospital when President Kennedy was pronounced dead. As soon as they heard the news, **Secret Service** agents rushed Johnson and his wife back to the presidential aeroplane to protect him. About an hour later, Mrs Kennedy arrived at the plane with her husband's body, which had been sealed in a coffin. A **federal** judge, Sarah Hughes, came to the aeroplane and swore the vice-president into office. Lyndon B. Johnson was now president of the United States.

The funeral

A funeral was held for John F. Kennedy on 25 November 1963. A horse-drawn cart pulled his coffin through the streets of Washington, D.C., on its way to the funeral mass at St Matthew's Cathedral. A riderless horse, the symbol of a fallen warrior who will never ride again, walked alongside the cart.

Heads of state, including kings, presidents, prime ministers and other representatives from 92 nations, came to Kennedy's funeral.

Kennedy's solemn-looking three-year-old son, then known as John-John, bravely saluted the coffin as it passed in front of the mourning family.

John F. Kennedy was buried at Arlington National Cemetery in Virginia. On his grave is an 'eternal flame', a symbol Jacqueline placed there to remind the world that he gave his life for his country. Fuelled by an underground line of natural gas, the flame at Kennedy's grave always burns.

WORDS OF SORROW

Members of the president's staff were deeply saddened by his death. Robert McNamara, the secretary of defence during both the Kennedy and Johnson administrations, said of John F. Kennedy's death that the country *'had suffered a loss which it would take ten years to repair'* and that there was *'no one on the horizon to compare with the President as our national leader'*. Averell Harriman, who was assistant secretary of state for Far Eastern affairs, said Kennedy's influence was much like that of Franklin D. Roosevelt, who had been president from 1932 to 1945. Harriman said, *'No two presidents before had had world opinion and affection centered upon them as had Roosevelt and Kennedy. In both cases people abroad felt they had lost a personal friend.'*

The world reacts

In the days after the **assassination**, the people of the United States tried to understand what had happened. For days, television networks focused on coverage of the president's death and his funeral. They also played clips from his life, taken from Kennedy home movies, the home movies of his friends, and newsreels the television networks had on file.

People queued for hours to pay their respects at the graveside of a beloved president.

Americans were not alone in their grief. All over the world, people mourned President Kennedy's death. When news of the assassination reached Russia, which was part of the **Soviet Union** and an enemy of the United States in the **Cold War**, radios played funeral music for hours. In West Berlin, at least 60,000 people gathered to mourn the loss of the US president. The square where they gathered was later named after John F. Kennedy.

In Ireland, almost everyone stopped what they were doing to pray for the president and his family. They felt especially close to Kennedy, whose grandfather had gone to the United States from Ireland in 1849. In Rome, Italy, taxi drivers parked a taxi outside the American **Embassy** and propped a huge funeral wreath up against it. In Britain, memorial services for President Kennedy were held all over the country.

The loss of a friend

Telegrams to Mrs Kennedy began to flood the White House. Everyone from Queen Elizabeth II to Nina Khrushchev, the wife of the Soviet leader, sent her words of comfort. In France, President Charles de Gaulle watched as his nation mourned. He said, '*I am stunned. They are crying all over France. It is as though he were a Frenchman, a member of their own family.*' In Africa, one man walked ten miles to the American Embassy. Once there, he said, '*I have lost a friend and I am so sorry.*'

In West Berlin on the night of November 23rd, people quietly walked through the streets carrying torches to mourn Kennedy's death.

The Warren Commission

On 29 November 1963, President Johnson appointed a group to study Kennedy's **assassination**. US **Supreme Court** Justice Earl Warren was the head of this **commission**. The group was told by President Johnson to study everything they could about the assassination to find out whether anyone besides Lee Harvey Oswald could have been involved. They were also told to find out more about Jack Ruby's murder of Oswald. Everything was to be reported back to the president and the American people.

Members of the Warren Commission handed their lengthy report to Lyndon Johnson in a formal meeting.

The Warren Report

The members of the commission interviewed 552 witnesses. On 24 September 1964, the commission delivered its report to President Johnson. They concluded that Oswald and no one else was involved in President Kennedy's assassination. There was no **conspiracy**, they said. Many Americans disagreed with the published report. They saw many things in the report that did not seem to be explained by the commission's findings.

Conspiracy theories

Many people wondered if President Kennedy's assassination was the result of a conspiracy. Some people thought organized crime groups might be involved. After all, Robert F. Kennedy – the president's brother and US attorney general – was trying to get rid of the Mafia crime ring in the United States. Both Jack Ruby and Oswald had connections to people in the Mafia. Not only that – Oswald had lived and worked for a while in the **Soviet**

Union and his wife was Russian. Other people thought Fidel Castro might have had something to do with the assassination. Perhaps, they thought, he was getting back at Kennedy for the Bay of Pigs invasion and for the Cuban Missile Crisis. Still others wondered if Americans who hated Kennedy's **liberal** ideas might be involved. In particular, many Southerners did not like Kennedy's proposal for **civil rights legislation** that would give African Americans equal rights.

Little did Abraham Zapruder know that the film he took of Kennedy smiling and waving from the Dallas motorcade would become one of the most famous pieces of film in history.

The Select Committee on Assassinations

There were so many questions left unanswered that thirteen years later, in 1977, **Congress** formed another committee, called the Select Committee on Assassinations. Members spent two years going over the Warren Report and interviewing the witnesses who were still alive. They also used more up-to-date technology to study bullets and a tape recording made during the motorcade. This committee announced in 1979 that the evidence did indeed suggest the presence of a second gunman. However, they did not name any suspects.

THE ZAPRUDER FILM

On the day President Kennedy was to come to Dallas, Abraham Zapruder, a dress manufacturer, went to see him and took along his movie camera. Zapruder was standing near the schoolbook warehouse and filmed the motorcade as President Kennedy was shot. When investigators found out about the film, they took it. Later, the Warren Commission studied it frame by frame to see if it could help them solve the mystery of what had happened. The film helped investigators time the shots and also helped them to determine exactly where the president's limousine was when the shooting took place.

Innocence lost

When John F. Kennedy became president, a new decade was beginning, and Americans saw him as a leader who was ready to guide the country in a new direction. Many Americans planned to vote for him in 1964 to give him the opportunity to lead the country for four more years. The new **civil rights** bill he had presented to **Congress** gave them hope that he was on his way to carrying out the goals of his New Frontier **platform**.

His death, however, took away much of that hope. Many historians say that with Kennedy's **assassination**, the whole country lost its innocence. Instead of living in an exciting place where **reforms** were being made, Americans were suddenly living in a country where a president could be killed.

The president's assassination made Americans look at many things differently. When the Warren **Commission's** report was published, people began to question their government in a way they had not done before. They began to wonder if the government was keeping information from the people to serve its own interests.

President Kennedy was building up US forces to fight in the war between North and South Vietnam.

CHINA

NORTH VIETNAM
Hanoi

Gulf of Tonkin

Hainan Island (part of China)

LAOS

South China Sea

Ho Chi Minh Trail

THAILAND

CAMBODIA

SOUTH VIETNAM

Gulf of Thailand

Saigon

N
W E
S

0   km   250
0   miles   250

The Vietnam War

Americans also questioned the actions of their country when the government started sending more American soldiers to Vietnam. Presidents Eisenhower and Kennedy had both been involved in providing money and military advisers for South Vietnam, but by the time Johnson became president, things were getting much worse.

Robert F. Kennedy, shown here at a press conference, was a prominent political figure like his brother, John.

North Vietnam was a **communist** country supported by the **Soviet Union**. Since the United States feared the spread of communism from one country to another, it supported the anti-communist government of South Vietnam. More and more US soldiers were sent to South Vietnam to fight in a **guerrilla** war against the **Vietcong**.

Many Americans protested against US involvement in Vietnam. However, by 1965, the United States had sent more than 180,000 American soldiers to fight in South Vietnam. By the time the war ended in 1973 with the surrender of South Vietnam to Communist North Vietnam, the war had cost the United States about US$200 billion, and about 58,000 American soldiers had died there.

MORE ASSASSINATIONS

In 1968, Americans were again shocked when two more leaders who had pursued the goals of Kennedy's New Frontier were assassinated. On 4 April 1968, an **assassin** in Memphis, Tennessee, killed Martin Luther King Jr, the best-known civil rights leader of his time. Two months later, on 5 June 1968, John F. Kennedy's brother, Robert, was shot and killed in Los Angeles, California. At the time, Robert Kennedy was running for president.

Johnson's presidency

The Great Society

On 27 November 1963, just five days after President Kennedy was **assassinated**, Lyndon B. Johnson gave his first speech to **Congress** as president. Johnson told Congress and America that he wanted to see Kennedy's civil rights bill passed, saying, '*Let us continue the ideas and the ideals*' of President Kennedy. Johnson had a hard time getting the Senate to pass the bill, but he worked hard, and the Civil Rights Act of 1964 became law on 2 July 1964.

While Kennedy had called his political **platform** the New Frontier, President Johnson won the 1964 election on a platform called the Great Society. Unsurprisingly many of the goals of the New Frontier were included in the Great Society, including improved conditions in cities, an end to poverty and more money for education.

Johnson's vision was of a country where government helped people to help themselves. During his time in office, he established programmes to do just that.

Giving people a head start

President Johnson and his **cabinet** set up programmes to help people get jobs and the Head Start education programme for young children from poor homes. Johnson also proposed a law in 1965 to guarantee voting rights for African Americans. Another act, the **Civil Rights** Act of 1968, sought to end racial **discrimination** in the sale or rental of houses or apartments. The laws helped, but the country was still experiencing racial **unrest**. As races clashed, riots broke out in US cities, such as Detroit, Chicago and New York.

The war in Vietnam

The Vietnam War continued to be a problem for President Johnson. By 1968, more than 500,000 US troops were in South Vietnam. The war had divided the country, and those who were against the war protested regularly. As time passed and the war continued, more and more Americans began to wonder what would happen next. In 1968, Johnson surprised many by announcing that he would not run for re-election. He said that he felt he had become a symbol for the war and that perhaps a new leader would find a way out of it.

THE CIVIL RIGHTS ACT OF 1964

The Civil Rights Act proposed by President Kennedy in 1963 and made law in 1964 states the following: *'All persons shall be entitled to the full and equal enjoyment of the goods, services, facilities, privileges, advantages, and accommodations of any place of public accommodation, as defined in this section, without discrimination or segregation on the ground of race, colour, religion or national origin.'* It goes on to explain in detail that people may not be discriminated against in theatres, restaurants, hotels or other public places. Its goal was to establish the Great Society that the United States was meant to be.

Johnson's Great Society provided new opportunities for many people. When Americans think of the 1960s, though, they often do not think of the accomplishments of Kennedy or Johnson. Instead, they recall the shocking assassination of a beloved president, the much-debated war in Vietnam and a decrease in the nation's wealth and sense of security.

Protests against the Vietnam War increased during the 1960s. If Kennedy had lived, would US involvement have been any different?

The Kennedy legacy

Kennedy died without achieving all the goals of his New Frontier **platform**. Some of the goals were later pursued by Johnson. In his **inauguration** speech in January 1961, Kennedy recognized that it would take a long time to fulfil his promises. He said:

> 'All this will not be finished in the first hundred days. Nor will it be finished in the first thousand days, nor in the lifetime of this Administration, nor even perhaps in our lifetime on this planet. But let us begin.'

Those words gave great hope to many Americans. They wanted to see a changed world – a world of peace, where there was no more poverty and where all people were treated equally under the law. Kennedy knew it would not be easy and that it would take time to make that world.

In a proud moment in US history, astronaut Buzz Aldrin stood on the moon next to an American flag.

Men on the moon

One area where Kennedy's goals have been achieved, perhaps in more ways than he ever thought possible, is in the US space programme. In a speech on 12 September 1962, President Kennedy told an audience at Rice University in Houston, Texas, that one of his goals for the country was to begin an exploration of space.

In his speech that day, he said:

> 'This generation does not intend to founder in the backwash of the coming age of space. We mean to be a part of it – we mean to lead it. For the eyes of the world now look into space, to the moon and to the planets beyond, and we have vowed that we shall not see it governed by a hostile flag of conquest, but by a banner of freedom and peace.'

The American space programme moved quickly. Two milestones had already occurred in Kennedy's lifetime. On 5 May 1961, Alan Shepard became the first American to go into space. On 20 February 1962, John Glenn became the first American to orbit the Earth. Several years later, on 20 July 1969, *Apollo 11* astronauts Neil Armstrong and Edwin E. 'Buzz' Aldrin Jr walked on the surface of the moon.

Increased awareness

The **assassination** of President John F. Kennedy seemed to shake Americans out of a kind of sleep. In the years following his death, people began to look at their world in a more realistic way. They became more aware of the financial hardships of others, of **injustices** in society and what government could do about such problems. Kennedy had not been able to pursue his ideal of a New Frontier, but Americans now realized that they had the power to create a government that would achieve the goals that were important to them.

Many places in the world have been named in memory of Kennedy. This is the John F. Kennedy Center for the Performing Arts in Washington, D.C.

Timeline

1917	29 May	John F. Kennedy born in Brookline, Massachusetts
1940		Kennedy graduates from Harvard University
1941	7 December	Japanese attack Pearl Harbor in Hawaii; United States declares war on Japan on 8 December and enters World War II
1943	2 August	Kennedy's PT boat is cut in two by a Japanese ship; Kennedy is injured, but leads crew to safety
1945	6 August	United States drops nuclear bomb on Hiroshima, Japan
	14 August	Japan surrenders to United States, ending World War II
1946		Kennedy runs for **Congress** and wins
1952		Kennedy runs for US Senate and wins
1953	12 September	Kennedy marries Jacqueline 'Jackie' Bouvier
1957		Kennedy wins Pulitzer Prize for *Profiles in Courage*
1958		Kennedy re-elected to Senate
1960		Democratic Party **nominates** Kennedy for president; Kennedy elected 35th US President
1961	20 January	Kennedy **inaugurated**
	12 April	Soviet Yuri A. Gagarin becomes first man in space
	17 April	Bay of Pigs invasion fails
	May	Freedom Riders go to Montgomery, Alabama
1962	October	Cuban Missile Crisis
1963	July	Limited Nuclear Test Ban Treaty signed by Soviet Union, United Kingdom and the United States
	28 August	More than 200,000 people hold a **civil rights** Freedom March in Washington, D.C.
	22 November	President Kennedy **assassinated** in Dallas, Texas; Lyndon B. Johnson becomes president
	24 November	President's **assassin,** Lee Harvey Oswald, shot and killed by Jack Ruby
	25 November	President Kennedy's funeral
1964	2 July	Kennedy's civil rights bill passed by Congress
	24 September	Warren **Commission** reports that Oswald acted alone in assassinating the president
1965		United States starts sending combat troops to Vietnam
1968	4 April	Martin Luther King Jr assassinated in Memphis, Tennessee
	5 June	Robert Kennedy assassinated in Los Angeles, California
1969	20 July	American Neil Armstrong is first man to walk on the moon
1979		Select Committee on Assassinations reports that the assassination probably involved at least two gunmen

Glossary

ambassador   representative sent from one country to another

assassin   person who murders a political figure

assassination   murder of a political figure

boycott   refusal to do business with or engage in other activities with a person, business, organization or government

cabinet   group of advisers

campaign   course of action one takes to get votes

Central Intelligence Agency (CIA)   US government agency that collects information about the activities of criminal and terrorist groups around the world

civil rights   rights of personal liberty guaranteed to US citizens by the Constitution and by acts of Congress

Cold War   dispute between Western countries and Eastern Europe after World War II, in which they were political enemies but not actually at war

commission   group assigned to a specific duty

communist   person or state that follows a class-free system in which land and industry are owned by the state; follower of communism

Congress   elected government of the USA

conspiracy   secret plot to achieve a goal

debate   formal discussion that follows certain rules of procedure

democracy   type of government in which leaders are elected by the people

desegregate   stop separating people based on race

discriminate   treat someone a particular way because of his or her race, religion, gender or another characteristic

embassy   building in which ambassadors to another country have offices while they are in a host country

enforce   make sure a rule or law is obeyed

exile   person who has had to leave his or her country

federal   from or associated with the US government

guerrilla   soldier who fights or attacks as part of a small, independent group

inauguration   official ceremony held to swear someone into office

injustice   unfairness or taking away someone's rights

legislation   act of making laws; or, laws that are made

liberal   open-minded, favouring reforms and progress

minimum wage   smallest amount of money that can be paid to an employee legally

naval blockade   ships from a navy blocking entrance to a country's main ports to keep goods or people from getting in

nominate   name a person who will run for office

platform   plan of action to achieve a goal

popular vote   votes of the citizens of a country

radioactive fallout   dangerous particles that come out of nuclear bombs

reform   change from one policy to another, or any change in a policy

Secret Service   division of US Treasury Department whose members protect the president and his family, among other duties

segregate   separate or set apart by race or gender

Soviet Union   former collection of states in Eastern Europe, led by Russia; also called the USSR

Supreme Court   highest court in US legal system

unconstitutional   something that goes against the US Constitution

unrest   protests, rioting or other disturbances

veteran   person who has served in a war

Vietcong   communist-led army formed to fight the South Vietnam government

Index